50 Korean Noodle Dishes

By: Kelly Johnson

Table of Contents

- Jjajangmyeon (Black Bean Noodles)
- Bibim Guksu (Spicy Cold Noodles)
- Jjamppong (Spicy Seafood Noodle Soup)
- Naengmyeon (Cold Buckwheat Noodles)
- Kalguksu (Knife-Cut Noodle Soup)
- Japchae (Stir-Fried Glass Noodles)
- Milmyeon (Wheat Noodles)
- Kongguksu (Cold Soy Milk Noodles)
- Spicy Jjajangmyeon
- Mul Naengmyeon (Chilled Broth Noodles)
- Bibim Naengmyeon (Spicy Cold Noodles)
- Seafood Kalguksu
- Spicy Octopus Noodles (Jjukkumi Noodles)
- Mandu Guksu (Dumpling Noodle Soup)
- Chicken Kalguksu
- Budae Jjigae with Noodles (Army Stew)
- Spicy Pork Japchae
- Soy Sauce Naengmyeon
- Spicy Kimchi Kalguksu
- Glass Noodles with Vegetables (Vegetarian Japchae)
- Chewy Wheat Noodles in Spicy Sauce
- Gochujang Cold Noodles
- Sesame Noodles with Cucumber
- Anchovy Broth Noodles
- Spicy Tuna Noodles
- Bulgogi Japchae
- Clam Kalguksu
- Cold Udon in Korean Sauce
- Spicy Crab Noodles
- Stir-Fried Kimchi Noodles
- Sweet and Spicy Stir-Fried Noodles
- Beef Broth Kalguksu
- Spicy Squid Noodles (Ojingeo Noodles)
- Kimchi Bibim Guksu
- Gochujang Kalguksu

- Tofu Japchae
- Shrimp Naengmyeon
- Radish Water Naengmyeon
- Braised Beef Japchae
- Korean-style Spaghetti (Rose Noodles)
- Spicy Clam Noodle Soup
- Stir-Fried Spicy Seafood Noodles
- Oyster Kalguksu
- Mushroom Japchae
- Korean Ramen Stir-Fry
- Spicy Cold Soba Noodles
- Korean Curry Noodles
- Kimchi Udon Stir-Fry
- Spicy Sesame Buckwheat Noodles
- Perilla Seed Kalguksu

Jjajangmyeon (Black Bean Noodles)

Ingredients:

- 8 oz fresh noodles
- 1/2 cup pork belly, diced
- 1/2 cup black bean paste
- 1 cup vegetables (onion, zucchini, potato), diced
- 1 tbsp sugar
- 1 tbsp cornstarch slurry

Instructions:

1. Stir-fry pork, add vegetables, and cook until tender.
2. Add black bean paste, sugar, and water; simmer.
3. Thicken with cornstarch slurry. Serve over noodles.

Bibim Guksu (Spicy Cold Noodles)

Ingredients:

- 8 oz somyeon (thin wheat noodles)
- 2 tbsp gochujang (red chili paste)
- 1 tbsp soy sauce
- 1 tbsp sesame oil
- 1 tsp sugar
- 1 boiled egg, halved
- Sliced cucumber and kimchi

Instructions:

1. Cook noodles, rinse in cold water.
2. Mix sauce ingredients; toss with noodles.
3. Top with egg, cucumber, and kimchi.

Jjamppong (Spicy Seafood Noodle Soup)

Ingredients:

- 8 oz fresh noodles
- 1/2 cup seafood mix (squid, shrimp, clams)
- 1 tbsp gochugaru (chili flakes)
- 1 tbsp soy sauce
- 1 cup vegetables (cabbage, onion, carrot)
- 2 cups chicken or seafood stock

Instructions:

1. Stir-fry seafood and vegetables; add chili flakes and soy sauce.
2. Pour in stock, simmer. Serve over cooked noodles.

Naengmyeon (Cold Buckwheat Noodles)

Ingredients:

- 8 oz naengmyeon noodles
- 2 cups cold beef broth
- 1 tbsp vinegar
- 1 tsp sugar
- Sliced pear and cucumber
- Boiled egg, halved

Instructions:

1. Cook noodles, rinse in cold water.
2. Mix broth with vinegar and sugar.
3. Pour broth over noodles, top with pear, cucumber, and egg.

Kalguksu (Knife-Cut Noodle Soup)

Ingredients:

- 8 oz fresh noodles
- 1 chicken thigh
- 4 cups water
- 1 clove garlic, minced
- 1 cup zucchini, julienned
- 1 tsp soy sauce

Instructions:

1. Boil chicken in water with garlic until cooked. Shred chicken.
2. Add zucchini and soy sauce; cook noodles in broth. Serve with chicken.

Japchae (Stir-Fried Glass Noodles)

Ingredients:

- 8 oz sweet potato glass noodles
- 1/2 cup beef, sliced
- 1 cup mixed vegetables (carrot, spinach, bell pepper)
- 2 tbsp soy sauce
- 1 tbsp sesame oil

Instructions:

1. Cook noodles, rinse, and set aside.
2. Stir-fry beef and vegetables; mix with noodles, soy sauce, and sesame oil.

Milmyeon (Wheat Noodles)

Ingredients:

- 8 oz fresh noodles
- 2 cups cold beef broth
- 1 tbsp vinegar
- 1 tsp sugar
- Sliced cucumber and pickled radish

Instructions:

1. Cook noodles, rinse in cold water.
2. Mix broth with vinegar and sugar.
3. Serve noodles in broth with cucumber and radish.

Kongguksu (Cold Soy Milk Noodles)

Ingredients:

- 8 oz somyeon noodles
- 2 cups soy milk
- 1 tsp sesame seeds
- Sliced cucumber

Instructions:

1. Cook noodles, rinse in cold water.
2. Pour soy milk over noodles; garnish with sesame seeds and cucumber.

Spicy Jjajangmyeon

Ingredients:

- 8 oz fresh noodles
- 1/2 cup pork belly, diced
- 1/2 cup black bean paste
- 1 tbsp gochugaru (chili flakes)
- 1 cup vegetables (onion, zucchini, potato), diced
- 1 tbsp sugar
- 1 tbsp cornstarch slurry

Instructions:

1. Stir-fry pork, add vegetables, chili flakes, and cook until tender.
2. Add black bean paste, sugar, and water; simmer.
3. Thicken with cornstarch slurry. Serve over noodles.

Mul Naengmyeon (Chilled Broth Noodles)

Ingredients:

- 8 oz naengmyeon noodles
- 2 cups cold beef broth
- 1 tsp vinegar
- 1 tsp sugar
- Sliced cucumber and pear
- Boiled egg, halved

Instructions:

1. Cook noodles, rinse in cold water.
2. Mix broth with vinegar and sugar.
3. Serve noodles in broth topped with cucumber, pear, and egg.

Bibim Naengmyeon (Spicy Cold Noodles)

Ingredients:

- 8 oz naengmyeon noodles
- 2 tbsp gochujang (red chili paste)
- 1 tbsp sesame oil
- 1 tsp sugar
- Sliced cucumber and radish
- Boiled egg, halved

Instructions:

1. Cook noodles, rinse in cold water.
2. Mix sauce ingredients and toss with noodles.
3. Top with cucumber, radish, and egg.

Seafood Kalguksu (Knife-Cut Noodle Soup)

Ingredients:

- 8 oz fresh noodles
- 1/2 cup seafood mix (shrimp, clams, squid)
- 4 cups broth (anchovy or seafood stock)
- 1 clove garlic, minced
- 1 cup zucchini, sliced

Instructions:

1. Boil broth, add garlic and zucchini.
2. Add seafood and cook until done.
3. Cook noodles in broth and serve.

Spicy Octopus Noodles (Jjukkumi Noodles)

Ingredients:

- 8 oz fresh noodles
- 1/2 lb small octopus, cleaned
- 2 tbsp gochugaru (chili flakes)
- 1 tbsp gochujang (red chili paste)
- 1 tbsp soy sauce
- 1 cup vegetables (onion, bell pepper)

Instructions:

1. Stir-fry octopus with chili flakes, paste, and soy sauce.
2. Add vegetables and cook until tender.
3. Serve over cooked noodles.

Mandu Guksu (Dumpling Noodle Soup)

Ingredients:

- 8 oz fresh noodles
- 6 dumplings (mandu)
- 4 cups beef or chicken broth
- 1 clove garlic, minced
- Sliced green onion

Instructions:

1. Boil broth with garlic, add dumplings.
2. Cook noodles separately and combine in broth.
3. Garnish with green onion.

Chicken Kalguksu

Ingredients:

- 8 oz fresh noodles
- 1 chicken thigh
- 4 cups water
- 1 clove garlic, minced
- 1 cup zucchini, julienned
- 1 tsp soy sauce

Instructions:

1. Boil chicken in water with garlic until tender; shred chicken.
2. Add zucchini and soy sauce, then cook noodles in broth.
3. Serve with shredded chicken.

Budae Jjigae with Noodles (Army Stew)

Ingredients:

- 8 oz fresh noodles
- 2 cups chicken or beef broth
- 1/2 cup sausage, sliced
- 1/2 cup spam, diced
- 1 cup kimchi
- 1 tbsp gochujang (red chili paste)

Instructions:

1. Boil broth with sausage, spam, and kimchi.
2. Add gochujang and simmer.
3. Cook noodles separately, add to the stew, and serve.

Spicy Pork Japchae

Ingredients:

- 8 oz sweet potato glass noodles
- 1/2 lb pork, sliced
- 2 tbsp gochujang (red chili paste)
- 1 tbsp soy sauce
- 1 cup mixed vegetables (carrot, spinach, onion)
- 1 tbsp sesame oil

Instructions:

1. Cook noodles, rinse, and set aside.
2. Stir-fry pork with gochujang and soy sauce.
3. Add vegetables, cook until tender, and toss with noodles and sesame oil.

Soy Sauce Naengmyeon

Ingredients:

- 8 oz naengmyeon noodles
- 3 tbsp soy sauce
- 1 tbsp sesame oil
- 1 tsp sugar
- Sliced cucumber and scallion

Instructions:

1. Cook noodles and rinse in cold water.
2. Mix soy sauce, sesame oil, and sugar.
3. Toss noodles in the sauce and top with cucumber and scallion.

Spicy Kimchi Kalguksu

Ingredients:

- 8 oz fresh noodles
- 1 cup kimchi, chopped
- 4 cups chicken broth
- 1 tsp gochugaru (chili flakes)
- 1 clove garlic, minced

Instructions:

1. Boil broth with kimchi, garlic, and chili flakes.
2. Add noodles and cook until tender.
3. Serve hot with extra kimchi on top.

Glass Noodles with Vegetables (Vegetarian Japchae)

Ingredients:

- 8 oz sweet potato glass noodles
- 1 cup mixed vegetables (carrots, spinach, mushrooms)
- 2 tbsp soy sauce
- 1 tbsp sesame oil
- 1 tsp sugar

Instructions:

1. Cook noodles, rinse, and set aside.
2. Stir-fry vegetables with soy sauce, sesame oil, and sugar.
3. Toss vegetables with noodles and serve.

Chewy Wheat Noodles in Spicy Sauce

Ingredients:

- 8 oz wheat noodles
- 2 tbsp gochujang (red chili paste)
- 1 tbsp soy sauce
- 1 tsp sugar
- Sliced cucumber

Instructions:

1. Cook noodles and rinse in cold water.
2. Mix sauce ingredients and toss with noodles.
3. Garnish with cucumber slices.

Gochujang Cold Noodles

Ingredients:

- 8 oz cold noodles
- 2 tbsp gochujang
- 1 tbsp sesame oil
- 1 tsp vinegar
- Sliced radish and boiled egg

Instructions:

1. Cook noodles and rinse in cold water.
2. Mix gochujang, sesame oil, and vinegar into a sauce.
3. Toss noodles in the sauce and top with radish and egg.

Sesame Noodles with Cucumber

Ingredients:

- 8 oz noodles
- 2 tbsp sesame paste
- 1 tbsp soy sauce
- 1 tsp sesame oil
- Julienned cucumber

Instructions:

1. Cook noodles and rinse in cold water.
2. Mix sesame paste, soy sauce, and sesame oil.
3. Toss noodles in the sauce and top with cucumber.

Anchovy Broth Noodles

Ingredients:

- 8 oz fresh noodles
- 4 cups anchovy broth
- 1 clove garlic, minced
- Sliced green onions

Instructions:

1. Boil anchovy broth with garlic.
2. Cook noodles separately and combine with broth.
3. Garnish with green onions.

Spicy Tuna Noodles

Ingredients:

- 8 oz noodles
- 1 can tuna, drained
- 2 tbsp gochujang
- 1 tsp sesame oil
- 1 tsp soy sauce

Instructions:

1. Cook noodles and rinse in cold water.
2. Mix tuna with gochujang, sesame oil, and soy sauce.
3. Toss noodles with the spicy tuna mixture.

Bulgogi Japchae

Ingredients:

- 8 oz sweet potato glass noodles
- 1/2 lb bulgogi beef
- 1 cup mixed vegetables (carrots, spinach, mushrooms)
- 2 tbsp soy sauce
- 1 tbsp sesame oil

Instructions:

1. Cook noodles, rinse, and set aside.
2. Stir-fry bulgogi and vegetables in soy sauce and sesame oil.
3. Toss with noodles and serve.

Clam Kalguksu

Ingredients:

- 8 oz fresh noodles
- 1 lb clams, cleaned
- 4 cups chicken or anchovy broth
- 1 clove garlic, minced
- 1 tbsp soy sauce

Instructions:

1. Boil broth with garlic and soy sauce.
2. Add clams and simmer until they open.
3. Cook noodles in the broth and serve hot.

Cold Udon in Korean Sauce

Ingredients:

- 8 oz udon noodles
- 2 tbsp gochujang (red chili paste)
- 1 tbsp soy sauce
- 1 tsp sesame oil
- Sliced cucumber

Instructions:

1. Cook noodles, rinse in cold water, and set aside.
2. Mix gochujang, soy sauce, and sesame oil into a sauce.
3. Toss noodles in the sauce and garnish with cucumber.

Spicy Crab Noodles

Ingredients:

- 8 oz noodles
- 1/2 lb crab meat or whole crab, cooked
- 2 tbsp gochugaru (chili flakes)
- 1 tbsp soy sauce
- 1 tsp sesame oil

Instructions:

1. Cook noodles and set aside.
2. Stir-fry crab with chili flakes, soy sauce, and sesame oil.
3. Toss with noodles and serve.

Stir-Fried Kimchi Noodles

Ingredients:

- 8 oz noodles
- 1 cup kimchi, chopped
- 2 tbsp soy sauce
- 1 tbsp sesame oil
- 1/2 tsp sugar

Instructions:

1. Cook noodles and set aside.
2. Stir-fry kimchi with soy sauce, sesame oil, and sugar.
3. Add noodles and toss to combine.

Sweet and Spicy Stir-Fried Noodles

Ingredients:

- 8 oz noodles
- 2 tbsp gochujang (red chili paste)
- 1 tbsp soy sauce
- 1 tsp honey
- Sliced vegetables (carrot, bell pepper, onion)

Instructions:

1. Cook noodles and set aside.
2. Stir-fry vegetables, then add gochujang, soy sauce, and honey.
3. Toss noodles in the sauce and serve.

Beef Broth Kalguksu

Ingredients:

- 8 oz fresh noodles
- 4 cups beef broth
- 1/2 cup thinly sliced beef
- 1 clove garlic, minced
- Sliced green onions

Instructions:

1. Boil beef broth with garlic.
2. Add beef slices and cook until tender.
3. Add noodles and cook until soft. Garnish with green onions.

Spicy Squid Noodles (Ojingeo Noodles)

Ingredients:

- 8 oz noodles
- 1/2 lb squid, cleaned and sliced
- 2 tbsp gochugaru (chili flakes)
- 1 tbsp soy sauce
- 1 tsp sesame oil

Instructions:

1. Cook noodles and set aside.
2. Stir-fry squid with chili flakes, soy sauce, and sesame oil.
3. Toss noodles with the spicy squid mixture and serve.

Kimchi Bibim Guksu

Ingredients:

- 8 oz cold noodles
- 1 cup kimchi, chopped
- 2 tbsp gochujang (red chili paste)
- 1 tsp sesame oil
- Sliced boiled egg

Instructions:

1. Cook noodles, rinse in cold water, and set aside.
2. Mix kimchi with gochujang and sesame oil.
3. Toss noodles with the sauce and top with sliced egg.

Gochujang Kalguksu

Ingredients:

- 8 oz fresh noodles
- 4 cups chicken or anchovy broth
- 1 tbsp gochujang (red chili paste)
- 1 clove garlic, minced
- Sliced green onions

Instructions:

1. Boil broth with gochujang and garlic.
2. Add noodles and cook until soft.
3. Garnish with green onions and serve hot.

Tofu Japchae

Ingredients:

- 8 oz glass noodles
- 1 block firm tofu, cubed
- 1 cup mixed vegetables (carrot, spinach, bell pepper)
- 2 tbsp soy sauce
- 1 tsp sesame oil

Instructions:

1. Cook noodles and set aside.
2. Stir-fry tofu and vegetables, then add soy sauce and sesame oil.
3. Toss noodles with the mixture and serve warm.

Shrimp Naengmyeon

Ingredients:

- 8 oz buckwheat noodles
- 1/2 lb cooked shrimp
- 4 cups chilled broth (beef or vegetable)
- Sliced cucumber and boiled egg

Instructions:

1. Cook noodles, rinse in cold water, and set aside.
2. Arrange noodles in a bowl, add shrimp, and pour chilled broth.
3. Top with cucumber and egg.

Radish Water Naengmyeon

Ingredients:

- 8 oz buckwheat noodles
- 4 cups radish water kimchi
- Sliced radish, cucumber, and boiled egg

Instructions:

1. Cook noodles, rinse in cold water, and set aside.
2. Arrange noodles in a bowl and pour chilled radish water kimchi.
3. Top with sliced radish, cucumber, and egg.

Braised Beef Japchae

Ingredients:

- 8 oz glass noodles
- 1/2 lb beef, thinly sliced
- 1 cup mixed vegetables (onion, carrot, spinach)
- 2 tbsp soy sauce
- 1 tsp sugar

Instructions:

1. Cook noodles and set aside.
2. Braise beef with soy sauce and sugar until tender.
3. Stir-fry vegetables, mix with beef, and toss with noodles.

Korean-Style Spaghetti (Rose Noodles)

Ingredients:

- 8 oz spaghetti
- 1 cup heavy cream
- 2 tbsp gochujang (red chili paste)
- 1 tbsp soy sauce
- Grated Parmesan cheese

Instructions:

1. Cook spaghetti and set aside.
2. Simmer cream, gochujang, and soy sauce to make a sauce.
3. Toss spaghetti in the sauce and top with Parmesan.

Spicy Clam Noodle Soup

Ingredients:

- 8 oz noodles
- 1 lb clams, cleaned
- 4 cups chicken or anchovy broth
- 2 tbsp gochugaru (chili flakes)
- 1 clove garlic, minced

Instructions:

1. Boil broth with gochugaru and garlic.
2. Add clams and simmer until they open.
3. Add noodles, cook through, and serve hot.

Stir-Fried Spicy Seafood Noodles

Ingredients:

- 8 oz noodles
- 1/2 lb mixed seafood (shrimp, squid, clams)
- 2 tbsp gochugaru (chili flakes)
- 1 tbsp soy sauce
- Sliced vegetables (onion, bell pepper, zucchini)

Instructions:

1. Cook noodles and set aside.
2. Stir-fry seafood and vegetables with chili flakes and soy sauce.
3. Toss noodles with the spicy seafood mixture.

Oyster Kalguksu

Ingredients:

- 8 oz fresh noodles
- 4 cups seafood or chicken broth
- 1/2 lb fresh oysters, cleaned
- 2 cloves garlic, minced
- Green onions

Instructions:

1. Boil broth with garlic, then add oysters.
2. Cook noodles in the broth until tender.
3. Garnish with green onions and serve hot.

Mushroom Japchae

Ingredients:

- 8 oz glass noodles
- 1 cup mixed mushrooms (shiitake, enoki, oyster), sliced
- 1 cup assorted vegetables (carrot, spinach, bell pepper)
- 2 tbsp soy sauce
- 1 tsp sesame oil

Instructions:

1. Cook noodles and set aside.
2. Stir-fry mushrooms and vegetables, season with soy sauce and sesame oil.
3. Toss noodles with the mixture and serve warm.

Korean Ramen Stir-Fry

Ingredients:

- 1 pack instant ramen
- 1/2 cup mixed vegetables (onion, cabbage, carrot)
- 2 tbsp gochujang (red chili paste)
- 1 tbsp soy sauce

Instructions:

1. Cook ramen, drain, and set aside.
2. Stir-fry vegetables, then add gochujang and soy sauce.
3. Toss ramen with the sauce and serve immediately.

Spicy Cold Soba Noodles

Ingredients:

- 8 oz soba noodles
- 2 tbsp gochujang
- 1 tbsp soy sauce
- 1 tsp sesame oil
- Sliced cucumber and sesame seeds

Instructions:

1. Cook soba noodles, rinse with cold water, and set aside.
2. Mix gochujang, soy sauce, and sesame oil for the sauce.
3. Toss noodles in the sauce and garnish with cucumber and sesame seeds.

Korean Curry Noodles

Ingredients:

- 8 oz udon or wheat noodles
- 1/2 lb chicken or tofu, cubed
- 2 tbsp Korean curry powder
- 1 cup mixed vegetables (potato, carrot, onion)
- 2 cups broth

Instructions:

1. Sauté chicken or tofu with vegetables.
2. Add broth and curry powder, simmer until thickened.
3. Stir in noodles and serve warm.

Kimchi Udon Stir-Fry

Ingredients:

- 8 oz udon noodles
- 1/2 cup kimchi, chopped
- 1 tbsp gochugaru (chili flakes)
- 1 tbsp soy sauce
- Green onions

Instructions:

1. Cook udon noodles and set aside.
2. Stir-fry kimchi with chili flakes and soy sauce.
3. Add noodles, toss to coat, and garnish with green onions.

Spicy Sesame Buckwheat Noodles

Ingredients:

- 8 oz buckwheat noodles
- 2 tbsp gochujang
- 1 tbsp sesame paste or tahini
- 1 tsp sesame oil
- Julienned carrots and cucumbers

Instructions:

1. Cook buckwheat noodles, rinse with cold water, and set aside.
2. Mix gochujang, sesame paste, and sesame oil for the sauce.
3. Toss noodles in the sauce and top with vegetables.

Perilla Seed Kalguksu

Ingredients:

- 8 oz fresh noodles
- 4 cups chicken or vegetable broth
- 2 tbsp perilla seed powder
- 1 clove garlic, minced
- Green onions

Instructions:

1. Boil broth with garlic and perilla seed powder.
2. Add noodles and cook until tender.
3. Garnish with green onions and serve hot.